SCARED TO DEATH

①

THE VAMPIRE FROM THE MARSHES

Drawing: Mauricet
Script: Virginie Vanholme
Colour work: Laurent Carpentier
Cover colour work: Solid!

9th CINEBOOK
The 9th Art Publisher

Original title: Mort de Trouille – Le vampire des marais

Original edition: © Casterman, 2000
by Mauricet & Vanholme
www.casterman.com

English translation: © 2008 Cinebook Ltd

Translator: Luke Spear
Lettering and Text layout: Imadjinn sarl
Printed in Spain by Just Colour Graphic

This edition first published in Great Britain in 2008 by
CINEBOOK Ltd
56 Beech Avenue
Canterbury, Kent
CT4 7TA
www.cinebook.com

A CIP catalogue record for this book
is available from the British Library

ISBN 978-1-905460-47-2

9th CINEBOOK
The 9th Art Publisher

12:20, THE LAVIGNE HOUSEHOLD.

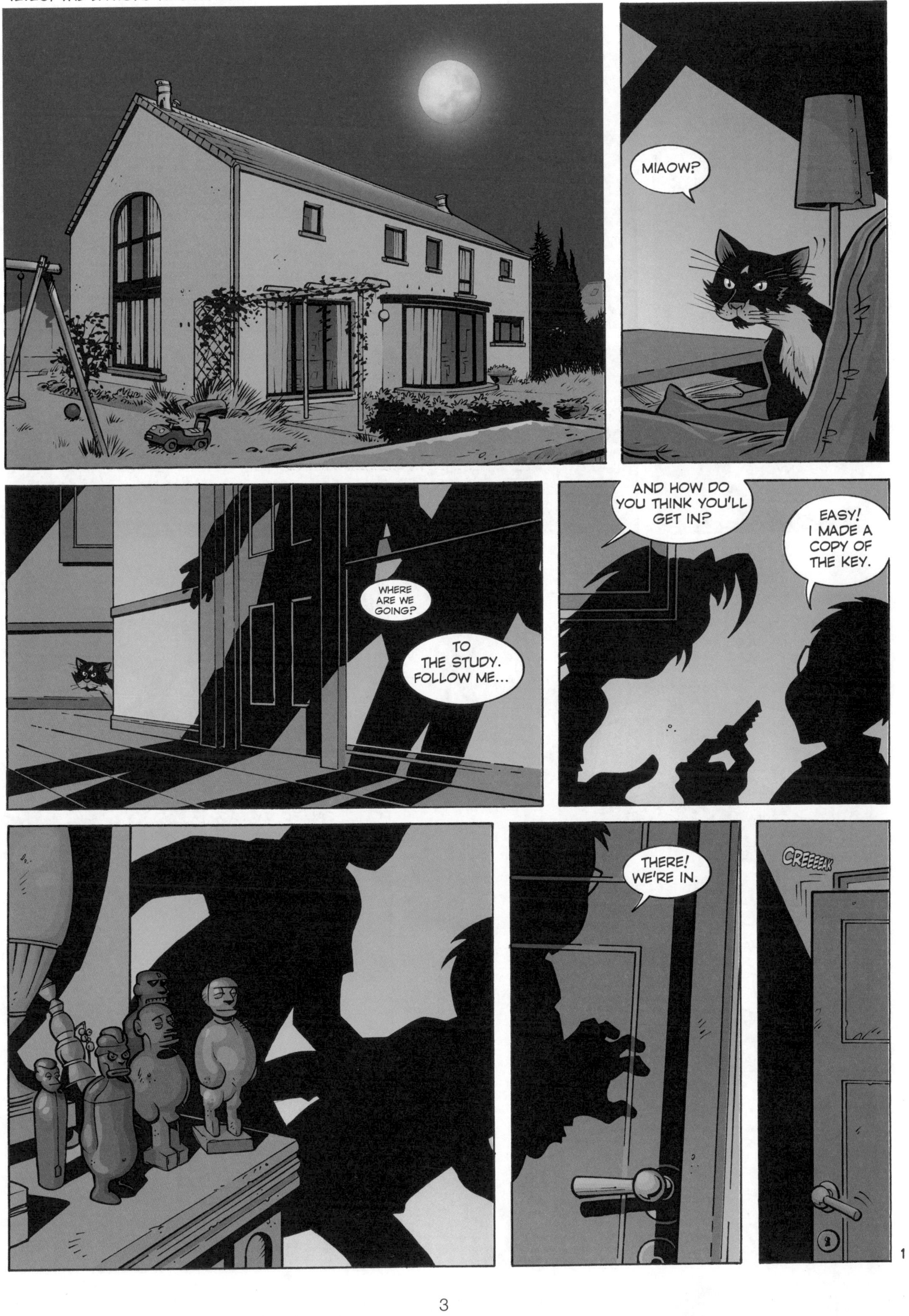
MIAOW?
WHERE ARE WE GOING?
TO THE STUDY. FOLLOW ME...
AND HOW DO YOU THINK YOU'LL GET IN?
EASY! I MADE A COPY OF THE KEY.
THERE! WE'RE IN.
CREEEEAK

1

I CAN'T SEE A THING IN HERE!...

LET'S GET IN BEFORE ANYONE HEARS US.

WOW! LOOK AT THAT, ROBIN! A SKULL! IS IT REAL?!

IF YOU LIKE OLD BONES, THERE'S A WHOLE SKELETON IN THE WARDROBE ON YOUR LEFT.

BUT THE BIGGEST FRIGHT OF ALL IS IN THIS FILING CABINET!

MY DAD PUTS IT ALL IN HERE; HIS INVESTIGATION FILES, REPORTS, PHOTOS, LEGAL-MEDICAL EXAMINATIONS, ALL THE BEST BITS!

I HEARD HIM SAY THAT HE WAS WORKING ON A STRANGE CASE AT THE MOMENT...

GIVE ME A KISS, YOU!

SO, ROBIN... WHAT'S STRANGE ABOUT THIS BODY?

I DON'T KNOW; GIVE ME A MINUTE TO READ...

DID HE LOSE HIS HEAD?!

IN ANY CASE, IF THE POLICE CALLED MY DAD, IT'S BECAUSE IT WASN'T A NATURAL DEATH!

A BODY THAT THE POLICE FOUND DOWN BY THE SWAMP!

TA-DA! THIS IS WHAT WE'RE LOOKING FOR.

DEADWATER SWAMP

4

THE MAN WAS DISCOVERED LAST TUESDAY, ALONG THE RIVERBANK BEHIND THIS BIG ROCK...

WOW! COOL! PHOTOS?!

HIS BODY WAS HIDDEN AMONGST THE REEDS.

GIVE THEM HERE, ROBIN!

SNAP

STOP IT, IDIOT! YOU'LL WRECK THEM!

WELL, YOU ONLY HAVE TO PHOTOCOPY THEM AND WE CAN GO BACK TO BED.

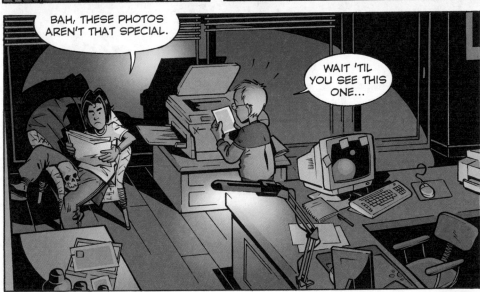

BAH, THESE PHOTOS AREN'T THAT SPECIAL.

WAIT 'TIL YOU SEE THIS ONE...

GOOD GRIEF!

DID YOU SEE ALL THOSE HOLES?!

MAX! WATCH OUT, THE SKU...

KRACK
ZBOING

OOPS! LET'S GET OUT OF HERE BEFORE YOUR DAD CATCHES US.

DON'T WORRY! HE WORKS SO MUCH NOWADAYS THAT HE SLEEPS LIKE A ROCK...

3

THE VAMPIRE FROM THE MARSHES

HELLO, DOCTOR LAVIGNE. WE WAITED FOR YOU BEFORE WE TOOK THE EVIDENCE.

TELL ME... DO A LOT OF PEOPLE COME DOWN HERE?

OH, WITH THIS BEAUTIFUL SUNSHINE THERE'S NO SHORTAGE OF PEOPLE OUT WALKING... IT WAS A JOGGER WHO DISCOVERED THE BODY, THIS MORNING AROUND 7:30...

AND AS OUR RUNNER TAKES THE SAME ROUTE EVERY DAY, WE CAN DEDUCE THAT THE BODY IS FRESH... WELL, IN A MANNER OF SPEAKING.

THE GUY WAS SO FULL OF ALCOHOL THAT HE MUSTN'T HAVE HEARD HIS ATTACKER APPROACHING.

HMMM... LET'S SEE THIS BODY.

INDEED... THIS DEATH IS QUITE UNUSUAL!

TERRIBLE, ISN'T IT? ALL THOSE HOLES... I WONDER WHAT WEAPON COULD HAVE DONE THAT?

MY FRIEND, ONLY AN AUTOPSY COULD TELL US THAT.

5

WHADDYAMEAN, NO AUTOPSY CONCLUSION?!

... THEY'RE MADE UP OF TWO PARTS, OR VALVES, WHICH PIVOT AROUND A JOINT... THE BIVALVES FEED BY FILTERING WATER. MUSSELS, FOR EXAMPLE, STICK TO PLACES WHERE CURRENTS BRING THEM PLENTY OF FOOD...

INVERTEBRATES

SHH! QUIET...

ARE YOU KIDDING ME? YOU CAN'T BE TELLING ME THAT THEY'VE GOT NOTHING ON THE CAUSE OF DEATH...

NOTHING... IF YOU DON'T BELIEVE ME, HAVE A LOOK FOR YOURSELF...

GO ON THEN, SHOW ME THE HORRORS!

BLERRR!

THAT'S SO GROSS! THAT STIFF MAKES ME SICK! I THINK I'M GONNA...

CRRRASH

INVERTEBRATE

MAX, I SUPPOSE? ...

WHAT WOULD YOU SAY TO A TIGHTROPE WALKING ROLE IN THE BARNUM & BAILEY CIRCUS?

UH-OH...

IT'D GIVE YOU A BIT OF BALANCE... AND YOU'D BE IN YOUR ELEMENT TOO, SURROUNDED BY CLOWNS AND MONKEYS!

HAHAHAHAHA

ERM... I'LL JUST GO STRAIGHT TO THE HEADMASTER, THEN?

2 HOURS OF DETENTION LATER...

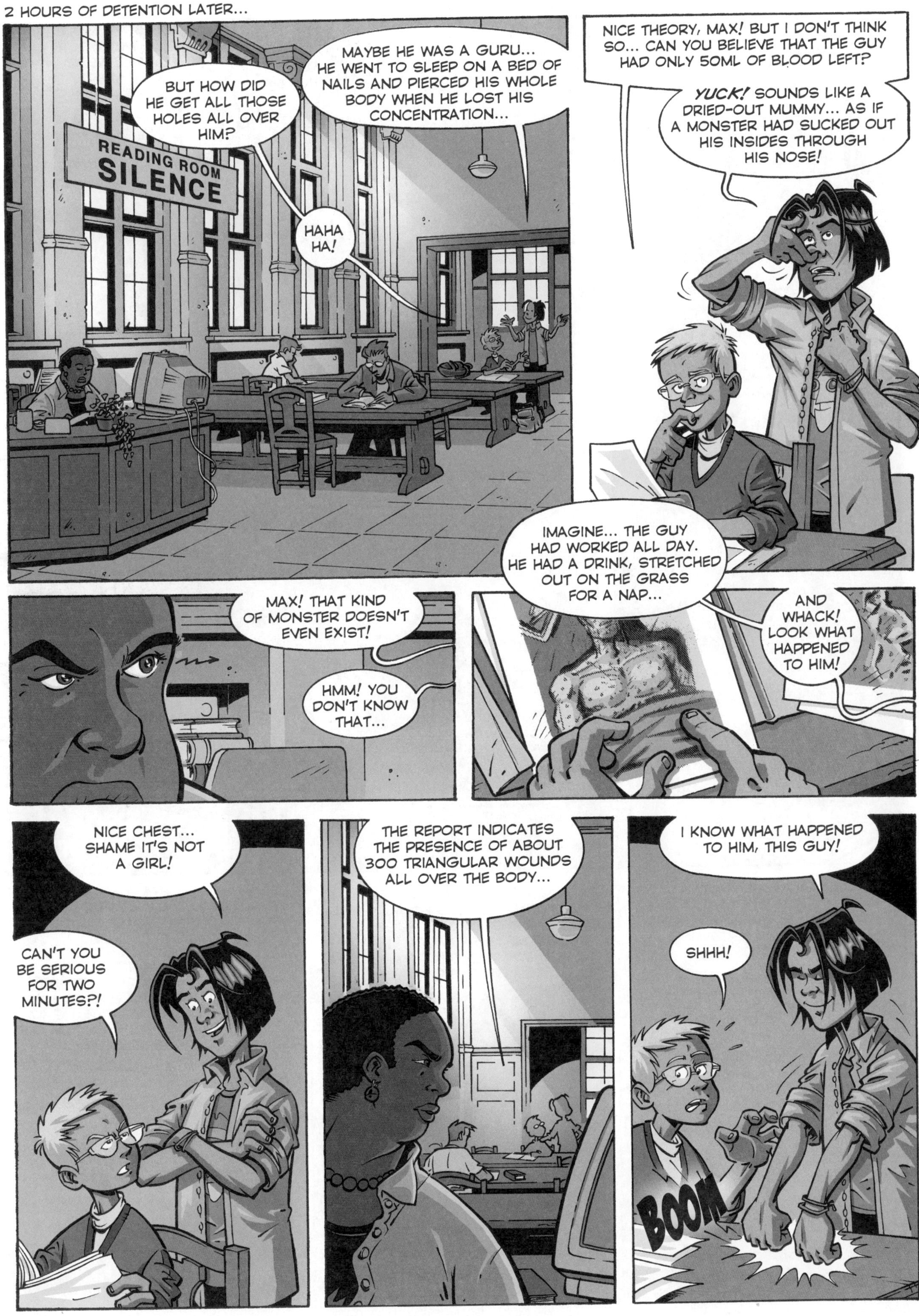

READING ROOM SILENCE
BUT HOW DID HE GET ALL THOSE HOLES ALL OVER HIM?
MAYBE HE WAS A GURU... HE WENT TO SLEEP ON A BED OF NAILS AND PIERCED HIS WHOLE BODY WHEN HE LOST HIS CONCENTRATION...
HAHA HA!
NICE THEORY, MAX! BUT I DON'T THINK SO... CAN YOU BELIEVE THAT THE GUY HAD ONLY 50ML OF BLOOD LEFT?
YUCK! SOUNDS LIKE A DRIED-OUT MUMMY... AS IF A MONSTER HAD SUCKED OUT HIS INSIDES THROUGH HIS NOSE!
MAX! THAT KIND OF MONSTER DOESN'T EVEN EXIST!
HMM! YOU DON'T KNOW THAT...
IMAGINE... THE GUY HAD WORKED ALL DAY. HE HAD A DRINK, STRETCHED OUT ON THE GRASS FOR A NAP...
AND WHACK! LOOK WHAT HAPPENED TO HIM!
NICE CHEST... SHAME IT'S NOT A GIRL!
CAN'T YOU BE SERIOUS FOR TWO MINUTES?!
THE REPORT INDICATES THE PRESENCE OF ABOUT 300 TRIANGULAR WOUNDS ALL OVER THE BODY...
I KNOW WHAT HAPPENED TO HIM, THIS GUY!
SHHH!
BOOM

7

HE WAS ATTACKED BY A BAND OF VAMPIRES WHO SUCKED OUT ALL HIS BLOOD! THOSE HOLES ARE REALLY *BITES*!

I SAW IT HAPPEN IN "THE VAMPIRE WHO CAME FROM MARS."

HAVE YOU BOYS NEARLY FINISHED WITH YOUR TOMFOOLERY? WE'RE IN A LIBRARY HERE!

COME ON... LET'S GET ON WITH IT.

WOW! THIS ONE LOOKS GOOD. LET'S TAKE IT!

THE TEETH OF THE ...HT

TOYBOX

DID YOU KNOW THAT THE VAMPIRE MYTH WAS ACTUALLY BASED ON A REAL PERSON?!

HMMM... INTERESTING BOOK YOU HAVE THERE. BRING THAT ONE TOO!

HUFF! PUFF!

VLAD III, ALSO KNOWN AS DRACULA, WAS A BLOODY WARRIOR WHO REIGNED IN THE 15TH CENTURY AS PRINCE OF WALLACHIE...

WALLAWHAT?

GRR!

BOOM

WALLACHIE! A PROVINCE IN ROMANIA. ACCORDING TO THIS BOOK, THE LIST OF HIS TORTURES WAS HUGE BUT HIS PREFERRED METHOD WAS IMPALING. THAT'S WHERE HIS NICKNAME CAME FROM: VLAD THE IMPALER...

HE WOULD HAVE MADE AN EXCELLENT HUSBAND FOR OUR BIOLOGY TEACHER...

BY DRINKING THE BLOOD OF HIS VICTIMS, DRACULA STARTED THE VAMPIRE MYTH, WHICH SPREAD THROUGHOUT EUROPE AT THE END OF THE 18TH CENTURY...

B

IF WE ARE TO BELIEVE THIS MAP, VAMPIRES APPEARED FOR THE FIRST TIME IN TRANSYLVANIA. THEN WE FIND TRACES OF THEM ALL ALONG THE DANUBE, A REGION RICH IN MARSHLAND...

AS IF BY CHANCE! VAMPIRES LOVE SWAMPS!

IN ANY CASE, I DON'T LIKE YOU BOYS!

141

14

GET OUT! I DON'T WANT TO SEE YOU HERE ANYMORE!

WELL DONE!

NOT A MINUTE TOO SOON!...

I'M TELLING YOU, ROBIN! IT ALL MATCHES UP! THE BODY WAS FOUND IN DEADWATER SWAMP, BLOODLESS AND BITTEN ALL OVER...

YEAAAH... I DON'T KNOW... THE HOLES SEEMED TOO SMALL TO BE INCISOR MARKS...

VAMPIRES WERE ABLE TO MUTATE OVER TIME, THEIR TEETH BECOMING SHORTER... OR MAYBE IT WAS CHILDREN. YOU KNOW, THE SON OF THE "VAMPIRE FROM MARS" HAD A LOT SMALLER TEETH THAN HIS DAD...

BUT IT'S POSSIBLE!

MAX! THAT'S PURE CINEMA...

RIGHT, SEE YOU TOMORROW.

THINK ABOUT IT, OKAY?!

COSMIC PATROL
RANGERS FEAR NO DANGER!

9

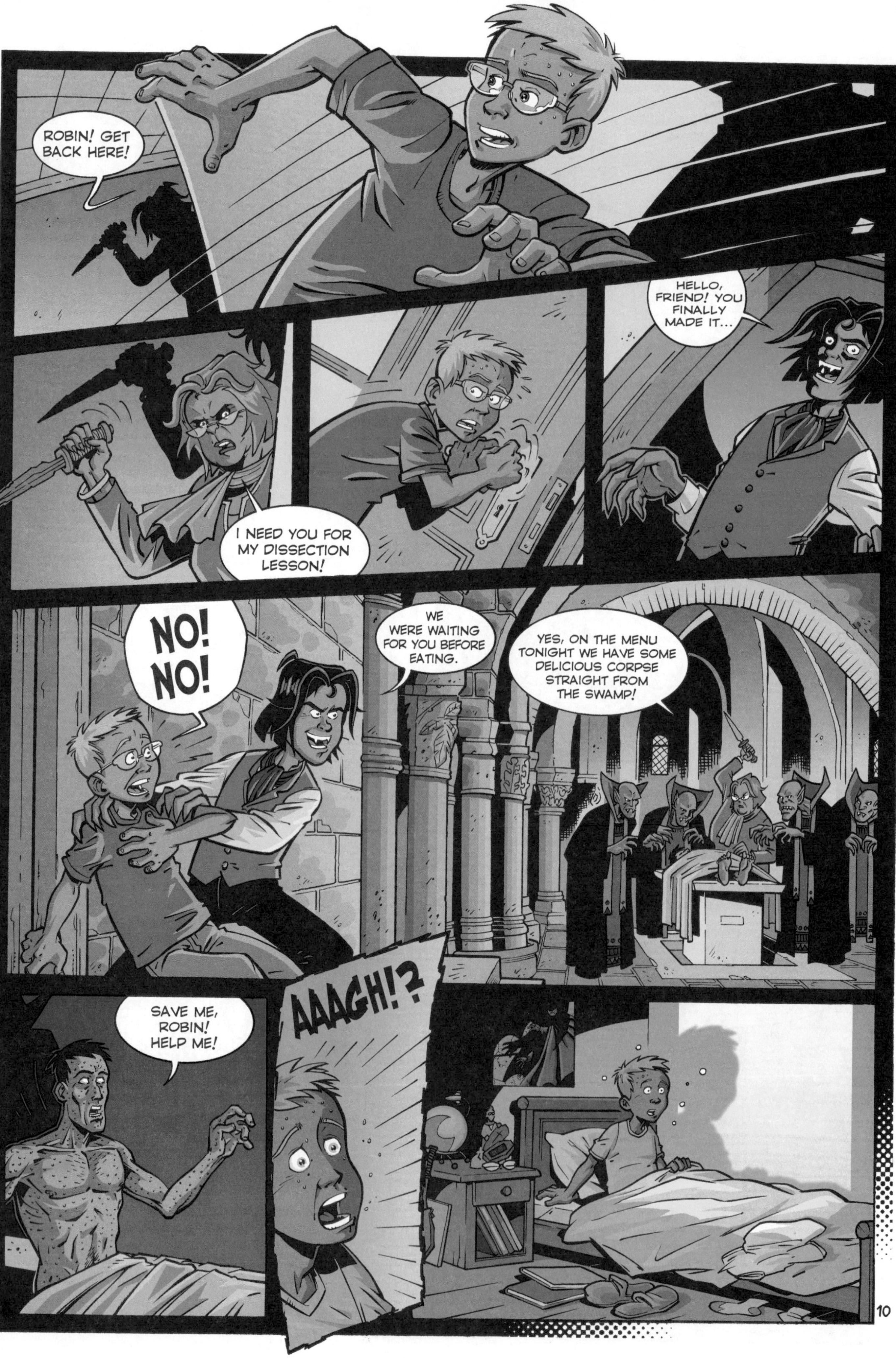
ROBIN! GET BACK HERE!
HELLO, FRIEND! YOU FINALLY MADE IT...
I NEED YOU FOR MY DISSECTION LESSON!
NO! NO!
WE WERE WAITING FOR YOU BEFORE EATING.
YES, ON THE MENU TONIGHT WE HAVE SOME DELICIOUS CORPSE STRAIGHT FROM THE SWAMP!
SAVE ME, ROBIN! HELP ME!
AAAGH!?
10

A LITTLE MORE COFFEE, DEAR?... BY THE WAY, I'LL HAVE TO SWING BY THE OFFICE THIS AFTERNOON...

YAWN!

SOPHIE, EAT YOUR TOAST!

BLEH!

YUM YUM

WHAT ABOUT YOU, ROBIN? YOU'RE NOT GOING TO EAT?

ERR... NO, I'M NOT VERY HUNGRY.

SAY, MUM, CAN I GET OUT OF DOING THE CLEANING?

DON'T WORRY! I'VE GOT ALL I NEED IN MY BACKPACK!... LATERS ALLIGATORS!

I PROMISED MAX THAT I'D MEET HIM AT 9 TO RIDE BIKES AND I'M RUNNING A LITTLE LATE...

ALL RIGHT, GO ON THEN! BUT AT LEAST TAKE SOMETHING FOR LUNCH!

"LATERS ALLIGATORS"?... WHERE ON EARTH DID HE GET THAT FROM?

FROM MAX, OF COURSE...

I DON'T LIKE THAT MAX TOO MUCH... ROBIN SHOULDN'T SEE HIM SO OFTEN.

"ON THE CONTRARY! IT CAN ONLY BE GOOD FOR OUR SON TO COME OUT OF HIS SHELL A LITTLE..."

11

SO, CHAMP? YOU DECIDED TO COME, DID YOU?

HUFF! PUFF!

I'VE GOT A NEW REPORT.

AND?...

IT WAS CONFIRMED THAT THE GUY DIED "...FOLLOWING HEAVY BLOOD LOSS..."

"FURTHER EXAMS WILL ESTABLISH THE EXACT CAUSE OF DEATH."

DO YOU REALISE WHAT THIS MEANS!?

WE'RE THE ONLY ONES TO HAVE FOUND OUT WHO THE KILLER IS. AND NOW... WE'RE GOING TO PHOTOGRAPH HIM!

YOU'LL SEE, WE'LL BE FAMOUS! WE'LL BE ON TV AND GIRLS WILL COLLECT OUR PHOTOS...

...IF WE'RE NOT "VAMPIRED" BEFOREHAND...

YOU SEE, YOU'RE STARTING TO BELIEVE!

BY COMPARING THE PHOTOS TO THE LOCAL MAPS, I WOULD SAY THAT THE CRIME SCENE IS... 300M TO THE LEFT.

THERE, DOWN THERE!... I RECOGNISE THAT ROCK.

YEAH! I CAN SEE THE POLICE TAPE!

12

14

... HERE WE ARE!

WOW! TO THINK THAT THE VAMPIRE WAS RIGHT HERE AND THAT IN ONE BITE... SNAP!

BUT WHICH WAY COULD HE HAVE RUN, AFTERWARD?

LOOKING AT THE AREA, THERE WASN'T THAT MUCH CHOICE... OVER THE BRIDGE, HE WOULD HAVE BEEN NOTICED STRAIGHT AWAY...

OVER THE WATER WOULD HAVE BEEN JUST AS OBVIOUS...

YEAAAH.... AND I CAN'T SEE A VAMPIRE COVERED IN BLOOD STROLLING PEACEFULLY AMONGST THE WALKERS.

NOPE!

HE MUST HAVE RUN OFF INTO THE UNDERGROWTH.

I'M SURE THAT HE'S STILL THERE!

13

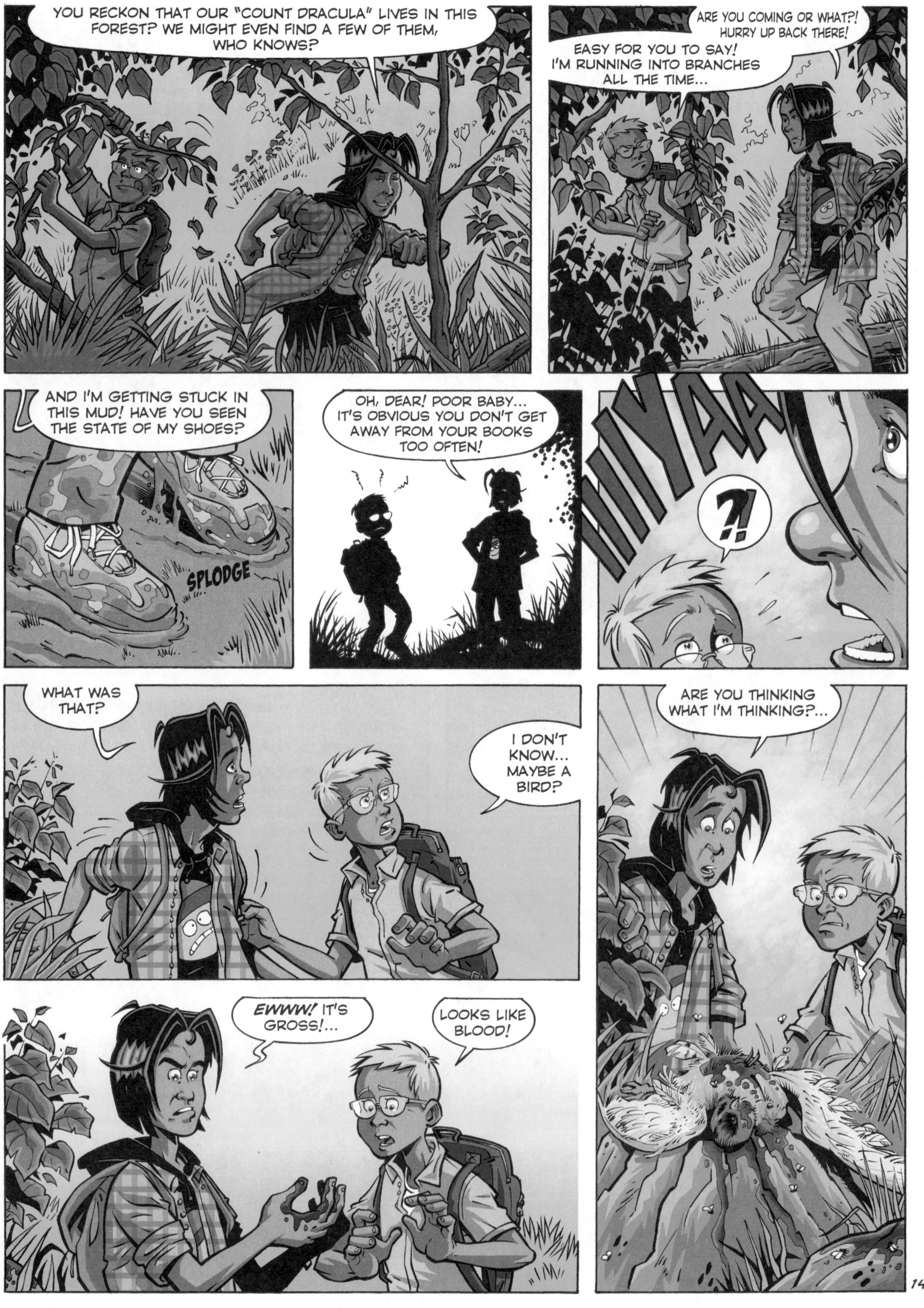
YOU RECKON THAT OUR "COUNT DRACULA" LIVES IN THIS FOREST? WE MIGHT EVEN FIND A FEW OF THEM, WHO KNOWS?
ARE YOU COMING OR WHAT?! HURRY UP BACK THERE!
EASY FOR YOU TO SAY! I'M RUNNING INTO BRANCHES ALL THE TIME...
AND I'M GETTING STUCK IN THIS MUD! HAVE YOU SEEN THE STATE OF MY SHOES?
SPLODGE
OH, DEAR! POOR BABY... IT'S OBVIOUS YOU DON'T GET AWAY FROM YOUR BOOKS TOO OFTEN!
IIIIYAA
?!
WHAT WAS THAT?
I DON'T KNOW... MAYBE A BIRD?
ARE YOU THINKING WHAT I'M THINKING?...
EWWW! IT'S GROSS!...
LOOKS LIKE BLOOD!
14

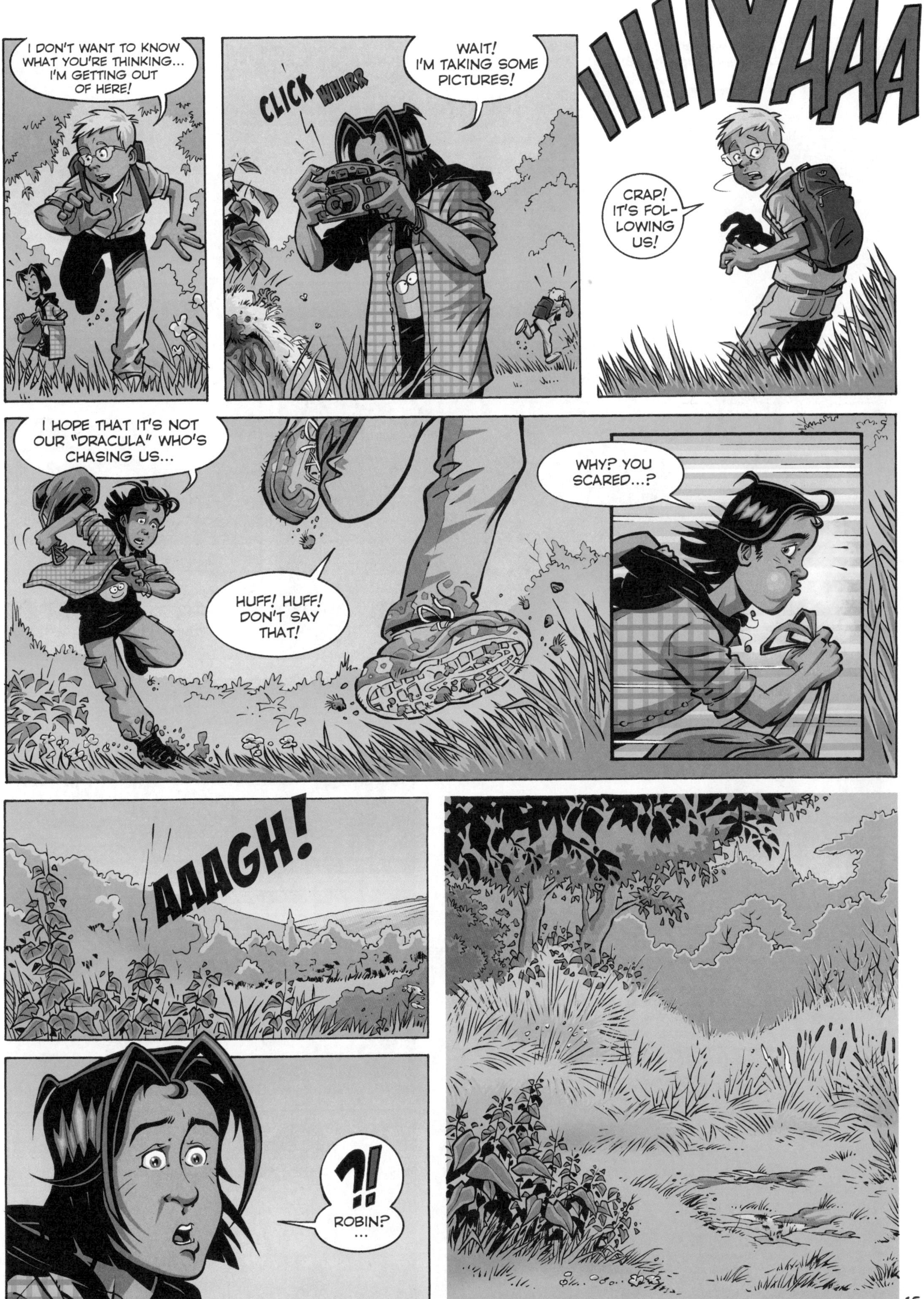
I DON'T WANT TO KNOW WHAT YOU'RE THINKING... I'M GETTING OUT OF HERE!
CLICK
WHIRR
WAIT! I'M TAKING SOME PICTURES!
IIIIIIYAAA
CRAP! IT'S FOL-LOWING US!
I HOPE THAT IT'S NOT OUR "DRACULA" WHO'S CHASING US...
HUFF! HUFF! DON'T SAY THAT!
WHY? YOU SCARED...?
AAAGH!
?!
ROBIN? ...

ROBIN, WHERE ARE YOU? ANSWER ME!

I'M HERE! STOP SHOUTING. YOU'LL GET US CAUGHT...

WELL, MATE! YOU FELL RIGHT INTO THAT TRAP...

BLOODY TRAP! HELP ME GET OUT OF HERE, WILL YOU.

CHEEP CHEEP

AND WHAT SHOULD WE DO WITH HIM?

CHIRP CHIRP

CHEEP CHEEP

WE'LL LET HIM GO.

SO, YOU BRATS!...

CHIRP CHEEP

?!

WHO GAVE YOU PERMISSION TO SET MY CALLER-BIRD* FREE?

WAAAAAH!!! THE VAMPIRE!

OTTO! GET 'EM, BOY!

GRRR

RUN!

* BIRD IN A CAGE THAT ATTRACTS OTHERS INTO THE POACHER'S NET WITH ITS SONG.

16

18

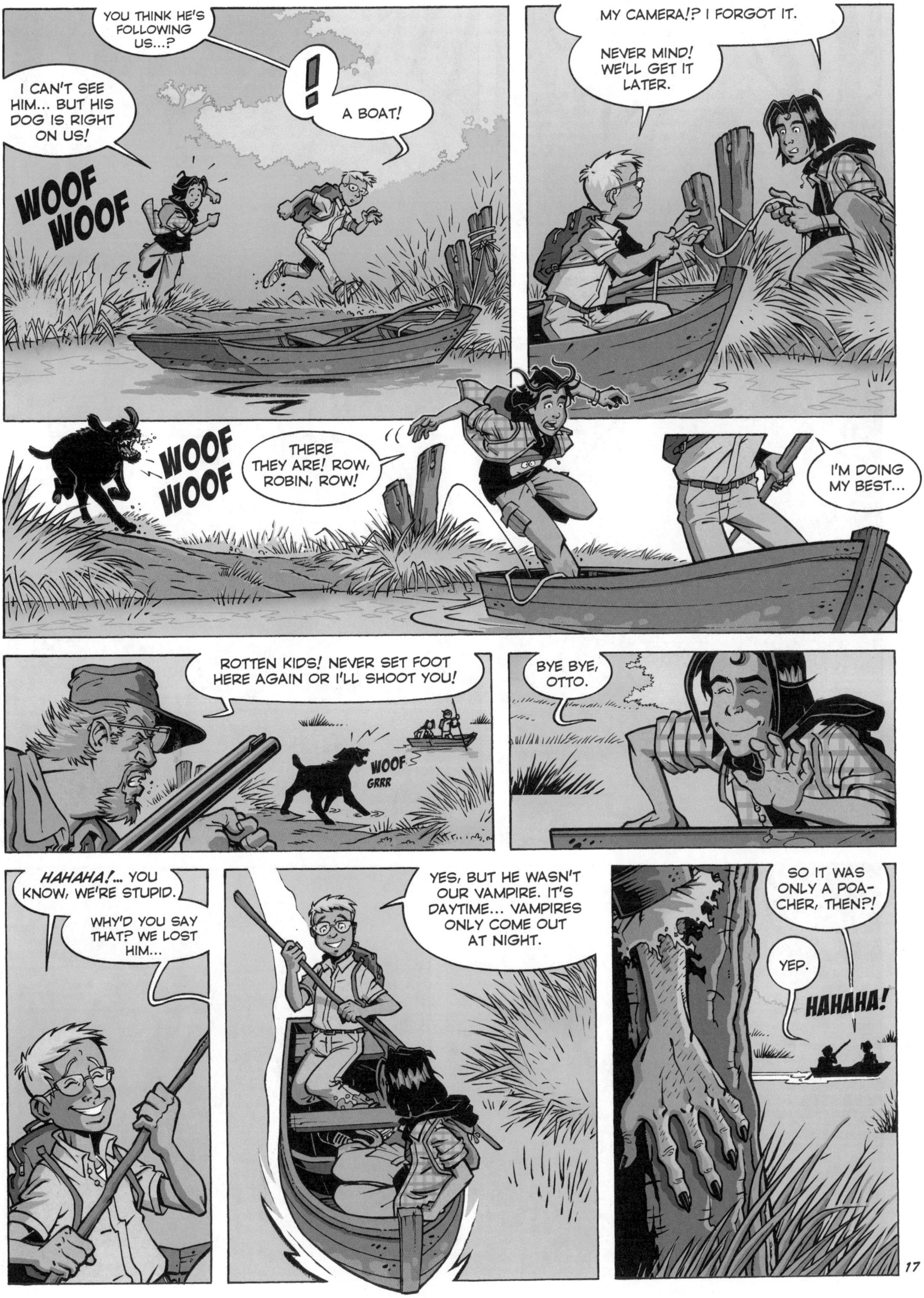
YOU THINK HE'S FOLLOWING US...?
I CAN'T SEE HIM... BUT HIS DOG IS RIGHT ON US!
WOOF WOOF
!
A BOAT!
MY CAMERA!? I FORGOT IT.
NEVER MIND! WE'LL GET IT LATER.
WOOF WOOF
THERE THEY ARE! ROW, ROBIN, ROW!
I'M DOING MY BEST...
ROTTEN KIDS! NEVER SET FOOT HERE AGAIN OR I'LL SHOOT YOU!
WOOF
GRRR
BYE BYE, OTTO.
HAHAHA!... YOU KNOW, WE'RE STUPID.
WHY'D YOU SAY THAT? WE LOST HIM...
YES, BUT HE WASN'T OUR VAMPIRE. IT'S DAYTIME... VAMPIRES ONLY COME OUT AT NIGHT.
SO IT WAS ONLY A POA-CHER, THEN?!
YEP.
HAHAHA!
17

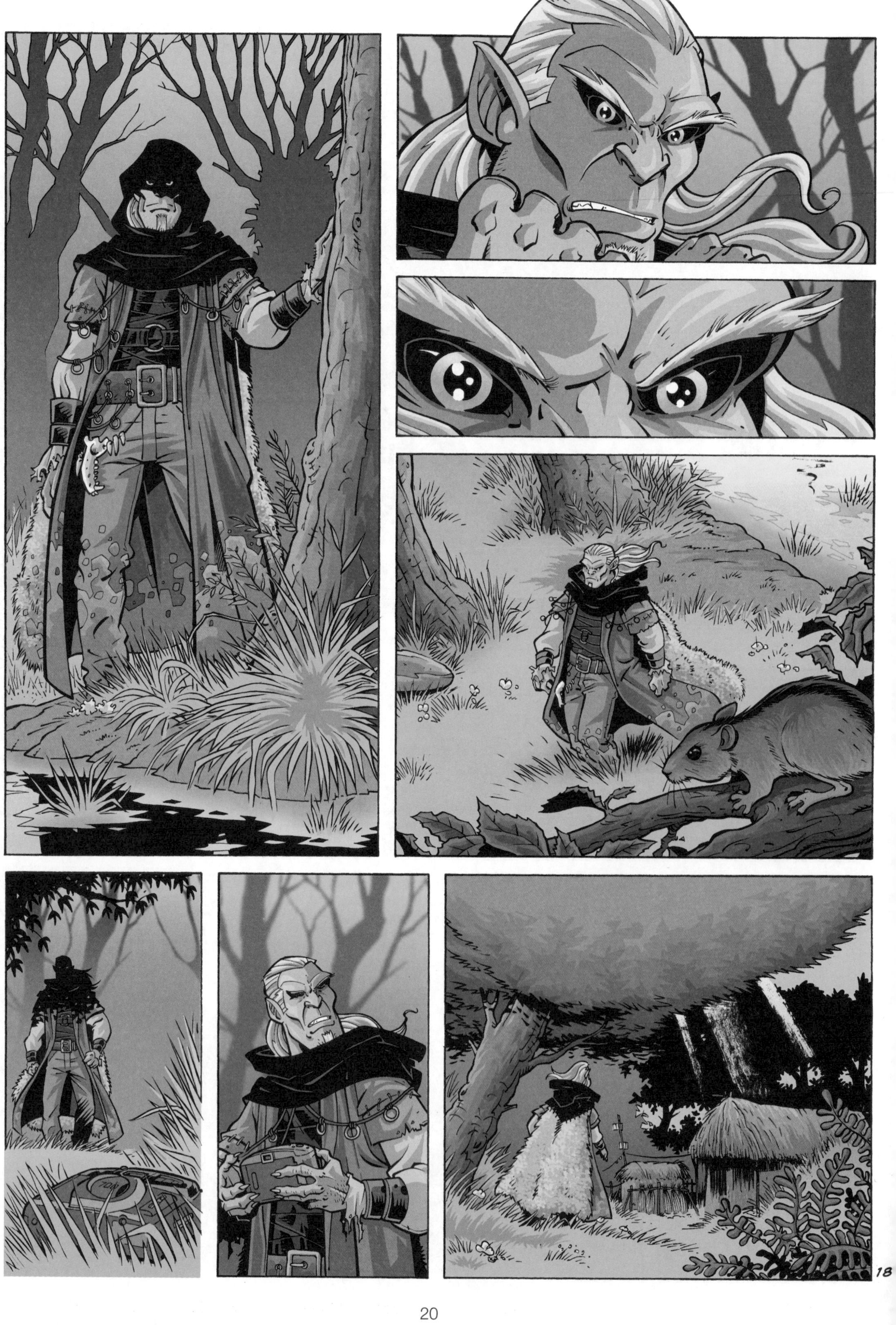
18

WHAT DID YOU SEE, JANUS...?

TWO BOYS... AROUND 14 YEARS OLD... THEY WERE CHASED AWAY BY A POACHER.

GIVE US THE DETAILS!

YES, TELL US! WHAT WERE THOSE KIDS DOING SO FAR OFF THE PATHWAYS?

I'VE SEEN KIDS SLIP INTO THE UNDERGROWTH BEFORE...

BUT THESE BOYS WEREN'T HERE TO BUILD A FORT...

NO! THEY SEEMED TO BE LOOKING FOR SOMETHING...

WHAT? YOU THINK THEY KNOW?!

CHEEP CHEEP

WE CAN'T BE SURE, BUT...

WE HAVE TO PROTECT OURSELVES!

CALM DOWN. LET'S NOT PANIC.

ALL RIGHT, BUT LET'S BE ON OUR GUARD...

SLURP!

CHEEP CHIRP

JANUS, YOU KNOW WHAT YOU HAVE TO DO.

19

WHO'S THERE? OF COURSE, I SHOULD HAVE KNOWN! IT'S YOU AGAIN...

VAMPIRE FROM MARS!

TREMBLE, JARVIS! I'LL PULVERISE YOU WITH MY PSYCHOTRONIC BLASTER. HAHAHA!

YOU CAN'T DEFEAT ME AS LONG AS I HAVE...

THE REMOTE CONTROL!

OH, DAD! JUST TWO MORE MINUTES, IT'S NEARLY OVER.

I'LL MISS THE NEWS WITH YOUR RUBBISH.

DIE, VAMPIRE!

CHANGE THE CHANNEL, PLEASE!

ON ONE CONDITION... MAX CAN SLEEP OVER NEXT WEEKEND.

GOOD GRIEF, IT'S A CLONE!

THAT'S ALL RIGHT BY ME. BUT YOUR FATHER CAN DECIDE...

SAY YES, DAD.

SO, DAD? CAN HE?...

THE THINGS YOU HAVE TO DO IN THIS HOUSE JUST TO SEE THE NEWS...

YEAH!

20

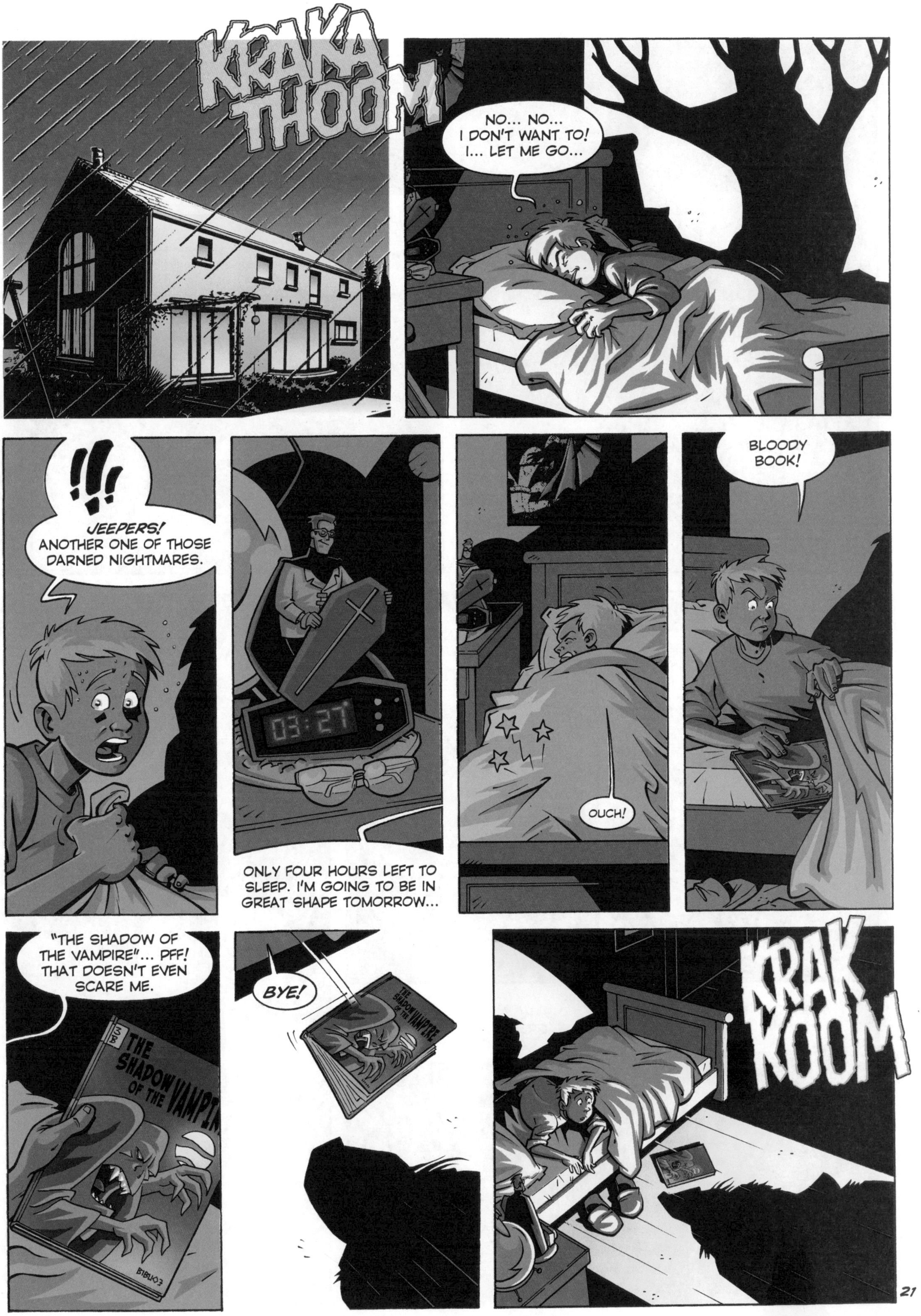
KRAKA THOOM
NO... NO... I DON'T WANT TO! I... LET ME GO...
!!!
JEEPERS! ANOTHER ONE OF THOSE DARNED NIGHTMARES.
03:27
ONLY FOUR HOURS LEFT TO SLEEP. I'M GOING TO BE IN GREAT SHAPE TOMORROW...
OUCH!
BLOODY BOOK!
"THE SHADOW OF THE VAMPIRE"... PFF! THAT DOESN'T EVEN SCARE ME.
THE SHADOW OF THE VAMPIR
BYE!
THE SHADOW OF THE VAMPIRE
KRAK KOOM

MUM!

WHAT'S WRONG? YOU'LL WAKE UP THE WHOLE HOUSE...

TH... THERE!

I SAW SOMEONE OUT THE WINDOW... IN THE TREE...

THERE, THERE, CALM DOWN.

HE... WAS FLYING!

I CAN'T SEE ANYTHING.

YOU THINK THAT ANYONE WOULD VENTURE OUT IN WEATHER LIKE THIS?

MAYBE DAD SHOULD GO AND LOOK...

BAH! YOU HAD A BAD DREAM, THAT'S ALL. AND REALLY...

24

SCHOOL
ETH SIMON
ENT PRIMARY
SECONDARY

IT WAS HIM! I'M SURE. HE FOLLOWED US.

I DON'T KNOW... I DIDN'T GET A GOOD LOOK.

WHAT?!... YOU DIDN'T GO TO THE WINDOW TO SEE?

WELL, ERRR, NO... I DIDN'T DARE.

I CAN'T BELIEVE IT. WHAT A WIMP!

SHUT UP! I'D LIKE TO HAVE SEEN YOU IN MY PLACE. YOU'D HAVE DONE THE SAME...

YOU DON'T GET SCARED, EH?

ME, NEVER!

HAHA HA

OOPS!

BOOF

SO WHAT'S THIS, THEN, IF YOU'RE NOT SCARED?

THAT THERE IS PREVENTION. A FEW ACCESSORIES, JUST IN CASE HE VISITS ME TOO...

DRIIIING

YEAH, YEAH... I DON'T KNOW IF I SAW A VAMPIRE, BUT IN ANY CASE, I DIDN'T GO BACK TO SLEEP.

I'M KNAC-KERED.

23

WAR WAS GENERALLY WAGED DURING THE SUMMER MONTHS. IT STOPPED WITH A COMMON AGREEMENT WHEN THE WEATHER DETERIORATED...

ROBIN?

SO THEY TOOK THEIR "WINTER QUARTERS." THE TROOPS FED THEMSELVES WITH FOOD FROM THE OCCUPIED LAND, WHENEVER THEY COULD...

ROBIN, ARE YOU SLEEPING?

DOESN'T TAKE MUCH.

I'VE GOT SOMETHING HERE THAT'LL WAKE YOU UP. WAIT...

JUST TAKE A LOOK AT THIS... THE LATEST "HUNTING AND FISHING."

YAAWN!

INSIDE, THERE'S FOUR PAGES ON TRAPPING TECHNIQUES... IT GAVE ME SOME IDEAS FOR OUR VAMPIRE.

THERE! YOU SEE? THEY EXPLAIN ALL THE IROQUOIS HUNTING METHODS...

MAX, WE'RE NOT IROQUOIS!... AND, WHAT'S MORE, WE NEVER WANTED TO HUNT THIS VAMPIRE...

BUT WE COULD TRAP HIM. WHAT DO YOU THINK? ISN'T THAT A GOOD IDEA?!

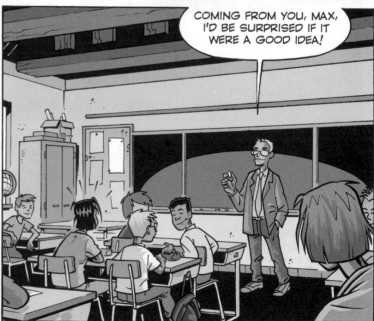

COMING FROM YOU, MAX, I'D BE SURPRISED IF IT WERE A GOOD IDEA!

2

I'M TELLING YOU, WE SHOULD TRY IT.

STOP NOW. YOU'VE BEEN HARPING ABOUT TRAPS ALL DAY...

COME ON, THEN... SHALL WE TRY?

THREE HOURS OF DETENTION ISN'T ENOUGH FOR YOU, EH? YOU WANT US TO RISK OUR LIVES, TOO?!...

BAH! YOU'RE EXAGGERATING... I'M SURE THAT WE CAN GET THIS VAMPIRE...

IT'S TRUE THAT MY BIG BRO EXAGGERATES ALL THE TIME!

!

WHAT ARE YOU DOING THERE?!

SOPHIE, ARE YOU SPYING ON US?

HI, MAX!

ERR... MUM SAID THAT YOU SHOULD WALK ME HOME TODAY, REMEMBER?

BUT I CAN GO HOME ALONE IF YOU WANT.

HEY, YOU'RE A LOT BRAVER THAN YOUR BROTHER!

COME ON, SOPHIE, LET'S GO HOME!

HUH? DON'T GET MAD, ROBIN!

LEAVE ME ALONE, YOU!

MOMO & NINIE 2000 - 25

SATURDAY NIGHT...

DING DONG

I'LL GET IT!

GOOD EVENING, MRS. MORNET. COME IN...

ARE THEY FOR ME?

GOOD EVENING, AND THANK YOU FOR YOUR INVITATION.

OH, IT'S ONLY RIGHT SEEING AS MAX WILL SLEEP OVER TONIGHT...

WHERE'S ROBIN, MR. LAVIGNE?

HE'LL BE RIGHT DOWN...

COME ON, LET'S GO TO THE LIVING ROOM.

COOL! YOU FOUND MR. SPOCK'S ANCESTOR!

AH! I SEE THAT YOU ARE INTERESTED IN PRIMITIVE ART. THAT MASK CAME FROM THE KROU TRIBE, IN CÔTE D'IVOIRE.

IT'S A VERY ANCIENT OBJECT. THERE'S SOMETHING MAGICAL ABOUT IT, WOULDN'T YOU SAY?

HAVEN'T YOU NOTICED ANYTHING STRANGE BETWEEN MAX AND ROBIN THESE DAYS?...

I WAS GOING TO TALK TO YOU ABOUT THAT. THEY SEEM TO BE A BIT COLD WITH EACH OTHER, DON'T THEY?

HERE COMES THE MOST HANDSOME!...

YOU TOOK YOUR TIME. YOU'RE WORSE THAN A GIRL!

YOU DIDN'T TELL YOUR FRIEND THAT WE'VE LIVED IN AFRICA?

HULLO, MISTER ROBIN.

DINNER TIME!

28

THE MEAL WAS REALLY DELICIOUS.

ONE DAY IN CAMEROON, I ATE A SKEWERED CRICKET KEBAB...

DON'T PUT US OFF OUR DESSERT, DEAR.

SO, ARE YOU STILL SURE YOU WANT TO CAMP OUT?

MORE THAN EVER! HAVE YOU ALREADY SET UP THE TENT?...

I SET IT UP THIS AFTERNOON, IN THE MIDDLE OF THE GARDEN.

THAT WAY WE'RE NOT TOO FAR FROM THE FRIDGE.

DON'T WORRY ABOUT YOUR BELLY...

I BROUGHT ENOUGH TO LAST US A MONTH!

AND WHILE THE ADULTS' EVENING ENDED...

GOODBYE!

SAFE HOME!

GOODNIGHT.

AND YOU TWO, NO MISCHIEF.

MAX AND ROBIN'S COULD BEGIN.

RIGHT, SOPHIE, OFF TO BED! YOU'RE WELL PAST YOUR BEDTIME... ME TOO, IN FACT.

I'LL COME OUT TO THE VERANDA WITH YOU, BOYS.

27

29

LIGHT THE WAY. I CAN'T SEE A THING!

STOP WHINING. YOU'RE ALREADY CARRYING THE LIGHTEST WEIGHT...

I'LL CLOSE THE DOOR BEHIND YOU.

BREAKFAST AT 9 TOMORROW. SLEEP WELL.

YEAH, RIGHT, THE LIGHTEST! I'D LIKE TO FEEL WHAT THAT BAG WEIGHS...

A TONNE, MY MAN!

I BROUGHT LOADS OF STUFF. CRISPS, POP, BINOCULARS AND... MY TRIGONOMETRY BOOK!

?!

NO... JUST KIDDING!... BUT I DID BRING THIS...

WHOA! THE SEQUEL TO "GREEN TERROR." IS IT ALREADY OUT?! WE'LL FINALLY FIND OUT WHAT HAPPENED TO COMMANDER BOB...

YEAH! HE WAS LOST IN THE AMAZON FOREST... I'M ON PAGE 35, JUST AT THE MOMENT WHERE HE DISCOVERS THE PESCAO VILLAGE.

ALL THAT'S LEFT ARE THESE BODIES RIPPED INTO A THOUSAND PIECES!

JEEZ!

WHAT BOB DOESN'T KNOW IS THAT AN EVIL SPIRIT IS LURKING IN THE JUNGLE... A KIND OF MONSTER, HUNGRY FOR HUMAN BLOOD.

THAT'S WHERE I AM. FOR THE REST, YOU'LL HAVE TO READ IT YOURSELF.

HAND IT OVER, NOW!

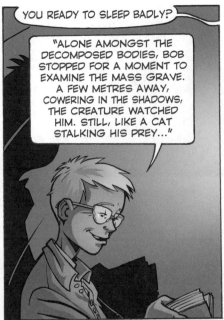

YOU READY TO SLEEP BADLY?

"ALONE AMONGST THE DECOMPOSED BODIES, BOB STOPPED FOR A MOMENT TO EXAMINE THE MASS GRAVE. A FEW METRES AWAY, COWERING IN THE SHADOWS, THE CREATURE WATCHED HIM. STILL, LIKE A CAT STALKING HIS PREY..."

"HIS FACE GAVE WAY ONLY TO HATE..."

"BOB'S STARE SHIFTED TO THE FOREST. NOTHING. NOT A SINGLE SIGN OF LIFE. THEN, ALL OF A SUDDEN, A STRANGE NOIS..."

CRACKK

CRUNCH

DID YOU HEAR THAT?!

DON'T WORRY! I BROUGHT SOMETHING TO PROTECT US.

MIAOW?

PHEW! IT'S JUST THE CAT.

STUPID ANIMAL!

! PFFRTTT MEOW

29

IT'S HIM, MAX! WE'RE DONE FOR!

IF WE GO OUT THAT WAY... BUT I HAVE AN IDEA!

GET READY. ON THREE, WE RUN TO THE KITCHEN DOOR...

MIAOOOW!

APOLOGISE TO YOUR DAD FOR ME, BUT WE HAVE NO CHOICE!

RIIIIP

HEY! THE TENT!... ARE YOU CRAZY?

?

THREE!

HELP!

HNNGH! I CAN'T OPEN IT!

HURRY!

I CAN'T BELIEVE IT. MY MUM HAS LOCKED US OUT!... DON'T LOOK. THERE'S NO KEY UNDER THE POT!

WHAT ARE YOU DOING?!

HMMPH

KLING

YOU'VE LOST YOUR MIND, MAX!

I DON'T WANT TO BE EATEN, MATE!

GOOD GRIEF! WHAT'S ALL THAT RACKET?! STAY THERE. I'LL GO AND SEE!

WHAT'S GOING ON OUT HERE?!

I HOPE THAT YOU HAVE A GOOD EXPLANATION...

?!

EEK!

I CAN'T QUITE BELIEVE IT... THAT SOMEONE WOULD BREAK A WINDOW TO ROB OUR HOUSE WHILE WE WERE THERE!

OH! YOU KNOW, DOC, NOTHING STOPS THEM NOWADAYS...

AND TO THINK THAT THE KIDS WERE OUTSIDE... HOW FRIGHTENING! THEY HAD A NARROW ESCAPE.

NO DOUBT ABOUT IT, HE KNOWS WHERE I LIVE...

YEAH! NEXT TIME, WE'LL HAVE TO GET HIM!

31

SO... NOW THAT YOU'VE BEEN ABLE TO SPY ON THEM, DID YOU FIND OUT WHAT THEY KNOW?

I DIDN'T HAVE TIME TO FIND THAT OUT, MOTHER... THAT CAT GAVE ME AWAY AT THE VERY MOMENT I WAS ABOUT TO APPROACH THEM...

AARGH! IF I COULD...

CALM DOWN, SON! CALM DOWN... WATCH OUT FOR YOUR METAMORPHOSES, BOY! LOOK WHERE THAT GOT THE OTHERS...

I KNOW, MOTHER. I SHOULDN'T GET CARRIED AWAY...

THE CHILDREN GOT AWAY WITH THEIR SECRET. I DIDN'T HEAR ANY OF THEIR CONVERSATION.

I FEAR FOR THE WORST. SOON WE'LL HAVE TO LEAVE...

SO THEY'LL NEVER LEAVE US IN PEACE?!

ANYWAY, THIS PLACE IS TOO BUSY NOW.

WITH ALL THESE WALKERS AND TOURISTS, IT'S NO LONGER POSSIBLE TO BE AT PEACE.

GO HOME AND REST. I'LL WARN THE OTHERS. WE'LL TAKE TO THE ROAD ONCE AGAIN...

32

34

THE NEXT DAY AT DAWN, MAX WENT BACK TO THE MARSH...

DETERMINED TO PUT HIS THREAT INTO ACTION.

PHEW, IT'S TOUGH! I'LL NEVER MANAGE TO DIG A HOLE BIG ENOUGH TO CAPTURE HIM...

HUMPH!

NEVER MIND, I'LL STOP THERE! WE'LL MAKE DO...

A BIT MORE OF THIS TO CAMOU- FLAGE IT ALL...

AND THE TRAP IS SET!

I'LL MAKE IT SO THAT HE STUMBLES INTO THE TRAP... AND ONCE HE'S IN IT, I'LL FINISH HIM WITH A FEW WHACKS FROM THE SHOVEL.

THE FINAL TOUCH: A CRUCIFIX AND GARLIC CLOVE NECKLACE!

RIGHT... WELL NOW, I JUST HAVE TO WAIT...

33

PFF! I'LL HAVE DESERVED THIS CATCH...

YAAAWN!

IS TIME STARTING TO DRAG A LITTLE FOR YOU?

?

BEING IMMORTAL, WHAT COULD I SAY TO THAT?

AAGH!

CRAAACK

SO, CAUGHT IN YOUR OWN TRAP? HAHAHA!

CRAP!

NO! DON'T HURT ME! DON'T... DON'T BITE ME, PLEASE!

YOU CAN OPEN YOUR EYES...

YOU'RE STILL ALIVE.

WE'RE... FLYING?!

LET ME DOWN! I... OR ELSE...

FORGET YOUR CROSS AND YOUR GARLIC... YOU'VE SEEN TOO MANY BAD MOVIES!

SAME FOR DAYLIGHT... IT'D TAKE A LOT MORE TO KILL A VAMPIRE!

WHERE ARE YOU TAKING ME?...

34

LET ME GO! I WANT TO GET DOWN!

YOU'RE OBSESSED WITH THAT...

BUT IF THAT'S WHAT YOU WANT!...

NO!

UNGH!

WHAK

"DON'T YOU WORRY!"

?!

YOU'RE WORRIED ABOUT MAX, EH?...

IF I WERE YOU, I'D GO DOWN TO THE SWAMP. HE SURELY NEEDS YOU...

HOW DO YOU KNOW THAT, NOSY PEST?!

HE'S YOUR BEST FRIEND! GO AND SEE HIM.

I WON'T TELL MUM AND DAD!

35

SUCK OUT ALL MY BLOOD?...

HMMMM...

WHAT ARE YOU GOING TO DO WITH ME?...

QUIET! DON'T TEMPT ME...

NO! I'M NOT THAT KIND OF VAMPIRE!

WHAT... KIND ARE YOU, THEN?

"I WAS BORN IN 1532 NEAR SAINT ANDREWS, A COASTAL TOWN TO THE EAST OF SCOTLAND. LIKE MY FATHER AND HIS FATHER BEFORE HIM, I WAS A FISHERMAN. MY LIFE WAS THE SAME AS OTHER FISHERMEN, MUNDANE AND SIMPLE..."

EVEN IF I'VE MUTATED SOMEWHAT OVER TIME, I AM WHAT MEN WOULD CALL A VAMPIRE.

"UNTIL THE DAY I CAUGHT A HEAVY LOAD IN MY NET..."

36

"TO MY GREAT SURPRISE I FISHED OUT A MOTIONLESS SHIPWRECKED BODY. IT WASN'T THE KIND OF CATCH I WAS USED TO..."

"HIS BODY SEEMED LIFELESS, AND WHAT'S MORE, SOMETHING DROVE ME TO BELIEVE THAT HE'D BE ALL RIGHT... IF I HELPED HIM. I DECIDED TO TAKE HIM HOME..."

"MY WIFE THOUGHT THAT HE'D ONLY BRING DRAMA AND DISASTER UPON OUR HOUSE. SHE AGREED NEVERTHELESS TO TEND TO HIM..."

"SEVERAL OF OUR LAMBS DISAPPEARED IN THE DAYS FOLLOWING THE STRANGER'S ARRIVAL."

"LINDA, MY DEAR AND TENDER COMPANION... YOU WERE RIGHT."

"HIS PHYSICAL FORM WAS FRIGHTENING AND HE GAVE OFF AN EVIL AURA. HE DIDN'T SEEM HUMAN!"

AS SOON AS HE'S ON HIS FEET, HE'LL LEAVE. I PROMISE YOU THAT.

HE SHOULDN'T HAVE SURVIVED. IT'S WITCH-CRAFT!...

"CURSED BE THE DAY WHEN I DRAGGED THAT CREATURE FROM THE WATERS IT WAS ROTTING IN!..."

NO!

"IT FIRST BIT MY SWEET LINDA..."

"THEN, IT WAS MY TURN."

"WHEN WE AWOKE, THE BEAST HAD ALREADY GONE. AND TO THANK US FOR HAVING SAVED HIM, HE GAVE US THE GIFT OF ETERNAL LIFE..."

"WE HAD ALSO BECOME VAMPIRES."

37

QUITE UNEXPECTEDLY, I QUICKLY GOT USED TO MY LIFE.

"THAT WASN'T THE CASE FOR LINDA... MY WIFE COULDN'T ACCEPT HER CONDITION AS A VAMPIRE. HUMAN BLOOD DISGUSTED HER..."

OH, NO, JANUS! SO YOU JUST CAN'T RESIST?!

GROAR

"ALL THAT WAS LEFT FOR HER WAS ANIMAL BLOOD..."

"STARVED, SHE WENT INTO A STABLE. THE POOR WOMAN WAS SO WEAK, SHE HAD TO FEED HERSELF..."

"OVERCOMING HER DISGUST, SHE BIT INTO A SHEEP'S NECK, FORGETTING THAT THE OWNERS COULD WALK IN AT ANY MOMENT..."

BAAAH
BAAAH
BAAAH
MOOO

"THE CRIES FROM THE CATTLE WOKE THE FARMER, WHO CALLED THE WHOLE VILLAGE."

A... A WITCH!

HELP!

KILL HER!

OVER THERE, IN THE BARN!

STOP HER!

WITCH! KILL HER!

"LINDA COULDN'T ESCAPE THE VILLAGERS' ANGER... EVEN TODAY, I REGRET NOT TRYING TO SAVE HER. BUT I WAS TOO TERRIFIED AT THE IDEA OF LOSING THIS ENDLESS LIFE THAT LAY BEFORE ME..."

WITCH!

TO DEATH!

BURN HER!

"LIKE A GOOD NUMBER OF VAMPIRES AT THAT TIME, LINDA BURNED AT THE STAKE."

"AS FOR ME, I TOOK TO THE ROAD, CHANGING INNS AS OFTEN AS POSSIBLE... ON THE WAY, I MET OTHERS LIKE ME."

"SOME OF THEM CHOSE TO LIVE IN SOCIETY. THEY HAD A PLEASANT TIME, ALL THE SAME."

"OTHERS, THOUGH, WANTED TO ESCAPE ALL TEMPTATION. THAT'S WHY THEY FOLLOWED ME... LIKE ME, THEY FED FROM ANIMAL BLOOD..."

"TODAY THEY ARE MY NEW FAMILY."

IT WOULD HAVE BEEN SO EASY TO KILL HUMANS FOR NOURISHMENT, BUT I COULDN'T DO IT...

IN SOME WAY I HAVE ACCOMPLISHED LINDA'S LAST WISH. SHE WHO NEVER WANTED TO BITE A HUMAN...

BUT... *SHH!* WE HAVE A VISITOR!

39

41

MAX! WHERE ARE YOU?

WHAT GOT INTO HIM, FOR HEAVEN'S SAKE?! WITH HIS STUPID VAMPIRE-HUNTING IDEAS!

MAX! ANSWER! I KNOW YOU'RE THERE!

?!

WH..WHERE AM I?

YOU FAINTED, MATE...

PFFF! I HAD ONE OF THOSE NIGHTMARES.

YOU WEREN'T DREAMING, ROBIN...

AH, YOU'VE FINALLY WOKEN UP? JUST IN TIME...I WAS ABOUT TO LEAVE. YOU CAN KEEP YOUR FRIEND COMPANY...

HEY! WAIT! WHAT'S GOING TO HAPPEN TO US?

BE QUIET AND YOUR LIFE WILL BE SPARED!

BUT IF YOU SAY ANOTHER WORD ABOUT US...

...I'LL COME BACK AND KILL YOU. FOR NOW, I'LL LEAVE YOU. I HOPE TO NEVER SEE YOU AGAIN!

40

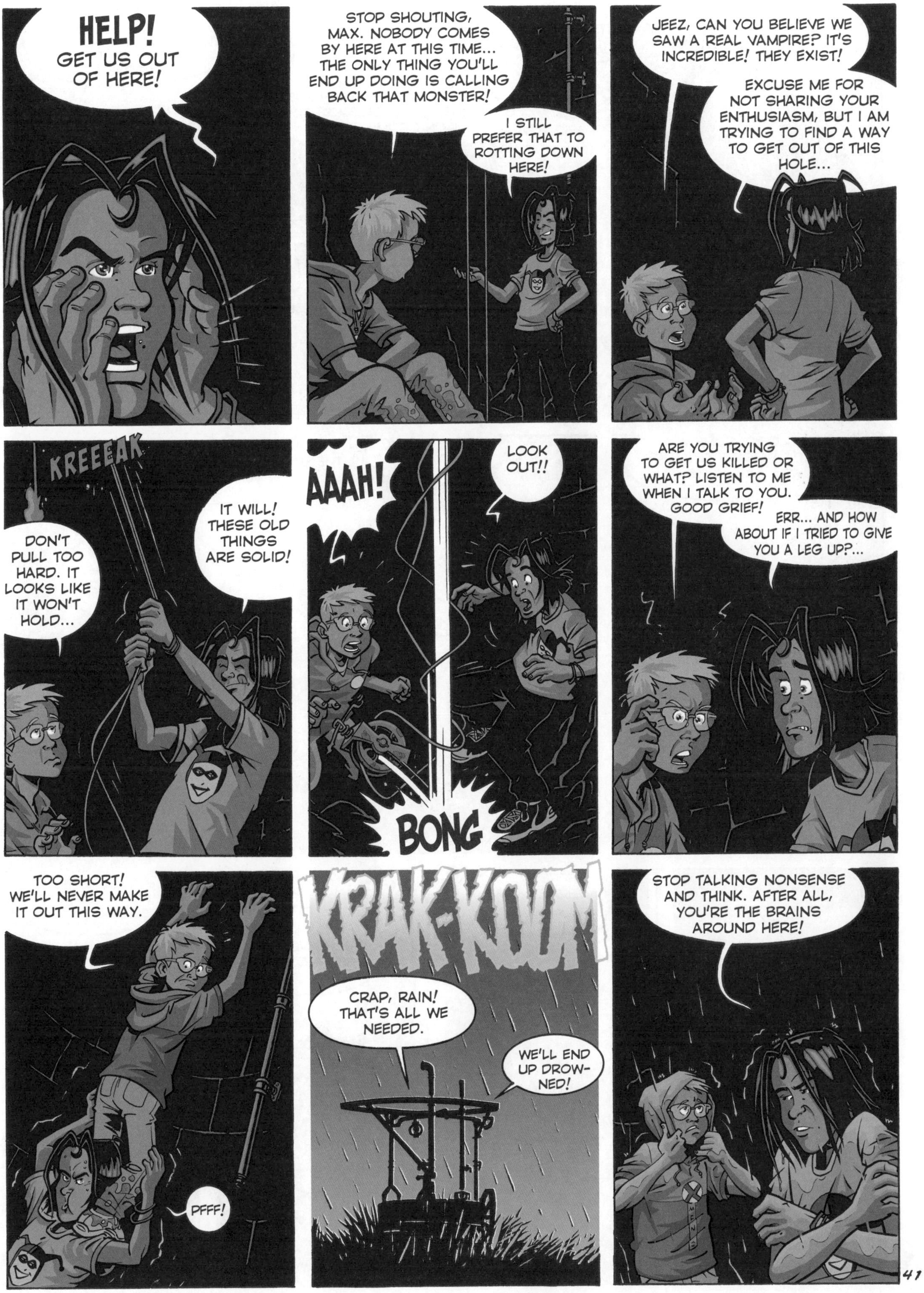
HELP! GET US OUT OF HERE!
STOP SHOUTING, MAX. NOBODY COMES BY HERE AT THIS TIME... THE ONLY THING YOU'LL END UP DOING IS CALLING BACK THAT MONSTER!
I STILL PREFER THAT TO ROTTING DOWN HERE!
JEEZ, CAN YOU BELIEVE WE SAW A REAL VAMPIRE? IT'S INCREDIBLE! THEY EXIST!
EXCUSE ME FOR NOT SHARING YOUR ENTHUSIASM, BUT I AM TRYING TO FIND A WAY TO GET OUT OF THIS HOLE...
KREEEAK
DON'T PULL TOO HARD. IT LOOKS LIKE IT WON'T HOLD...
IT WILL! THESE OLD THINGS ARE SOLID!
AAAH!
LOOK OUT!!
BONG
ARE YOU TRYING TO GET US KILLED OR WHAT? LISTEN TO ME WHEN I TALK TO YOU. GOOD GRIEF!
ERR... AND HOW ABOUT IF I TRIED TO GIVE YOU A LEG UP?...
TOO SHORT! WE'LL NEVER MAKE IT OUT THIS WAY.
PFFF!
KRAK-KOOM
CRAP, RAIN! THAT'S ALL WE NEEDED.
WE'LL END UP DROWNED!
STOP TALKING NONSENSE AND THINK. AFTER ALL, YOU'RE THE BRAINS AROUND HERE!
41

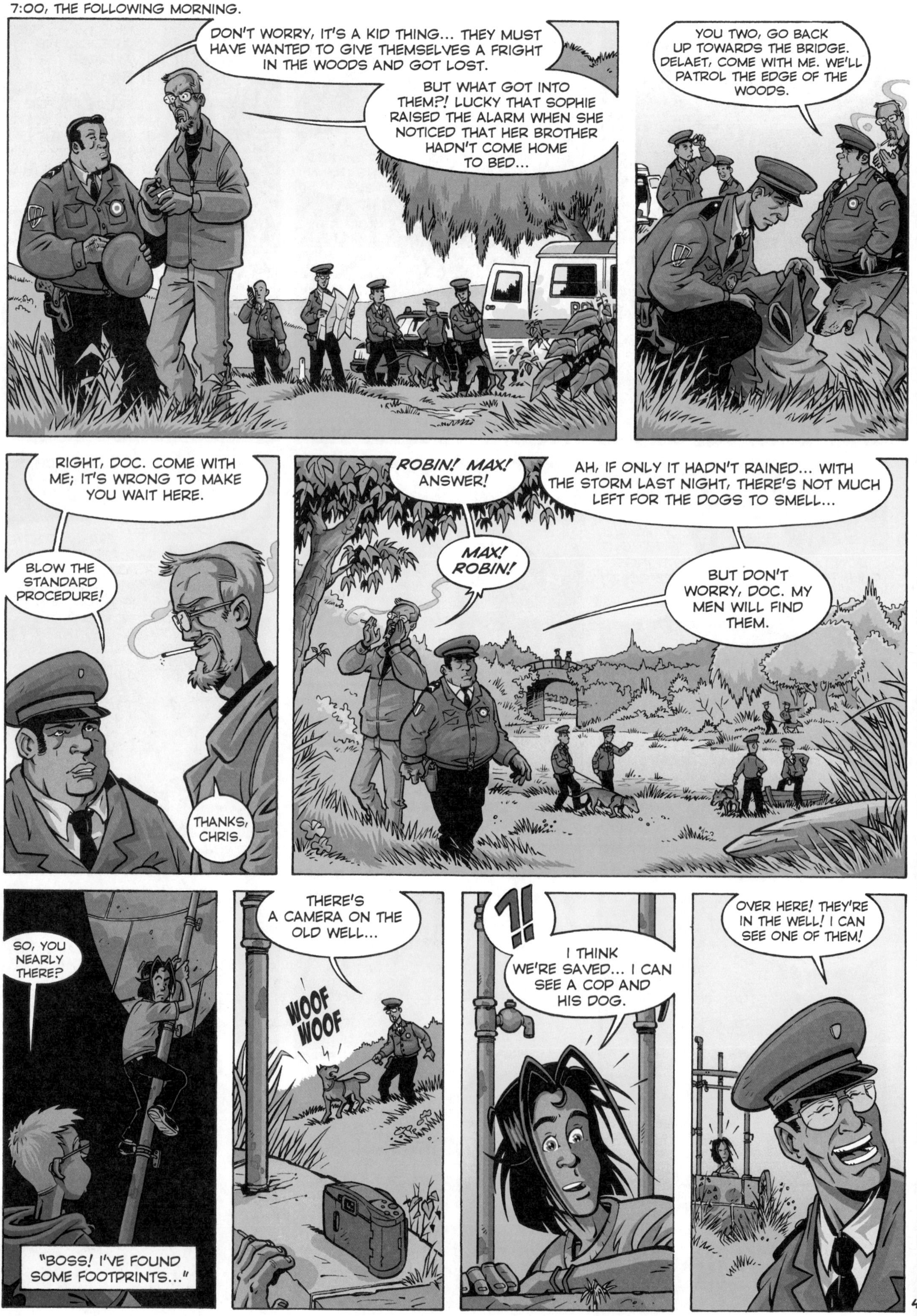
7:00, THE FOLLOWING MORNING.
DON'T WORRY, IT'S A KID THING... THEY MUST HAVE WANTED TO GIVE THEMSELVES A FRIGHT IN THE WOODS AND GOT LOST.
BUT WHAT GOT INTO THEM?! LUCKY THAT SOPHIE RAISED THE ALARM WHEN SHE NOTICED THAT HER BROTHER HADN'T COME HOME TO BED...
YOU TWO, GO BACK UP TOWARDS THE BRIDGE. DELAET, COME WITH ME. WE'LL PATROL THE EDGE OF THE WOODS.
RIGHT, DOC. COME WITH ME; IT'S WRONG TO MAKE YOU WAIT HERE.
BLOW THE STANDARD PROCEDURE!
THANKS, CHRIS.
ROBIN! MAX! ANSWER!
AH, IF ONLY IT HADN'T RAINED... WITH THE STORM LAST NIGHT, THERE'S NOT MUCH LEFT FOR THE DOGS TO SMELL...
MAX! ROBIN!
BUT DON'T WORRY, DOC. MY MEN WILL FIND THEM.
SO, YOU NEARLY THERE?
"BOSS! I'VE FOUND SOME FOOTPRINTS..."
THERE'S A CAMERA ON THE OLD WELL...
WOOF WOOF
?!
I THINK WE'RE SAVED... I CAN SEE A COP AND HIS DOG.
OVER HERE! THEY'RE IN THE WELL! I CAN SEE ONE OF THEM!

DON'T WORRY, YOUNG MAN. WE'LL HELP YOU UP.

MAX! WHERE'S *ROBIN?!*

HE'S STILL DOWN THERE. EVERYTHING'S OKAY.

WHAT ON EARTH ARE YOU DOING DOWN THERE?

RELAX, DOC!

THEY SPENT THE ENTIRE NIGHT IN THAT HOLE.

YOU'RE COMPLETELY INSANE! WHAT GOT INTO YOU?...

I'M SORRY, DAD. IF I'D KNOWN HOW WE'D END UP, I WOULD HAVE NEVER LOOKED IN YOUR FILES...

MY FILES? WHAT ARE YOU TALKING ABOUT?

YOUR MEDICAL-LEGAL REPORTS...

YOU'VE BEEN POKING AROUND MY OFFICE?

IT'S ALL MY FAULT, SIR. I READ IN THE PAPER ABOUT A GUY FOUND DEAD NOT FAR FROM HERE. THE ARTICLE MENTIONED THAT IT WAS A STRANGE MURDER, WORTHY OF A VAMPIRE BOOK. THAT INTRIGUED US, AND AS YOU WERE ON THE CASE...

WHAT'S ALL THIS NONSENSE? THAT MAN DIED OF NATURAL CAUSES. NO VAMPIRES... BIT HIM, OR WHATEVER ELSE!!

THE POOR MAN WAS ATTACKED BY A MASS OF LEECHES. HE MUST HAVE GONE A LITTLE HEAVY ON THE BOTTLE, POOR BUGGER. THE FACT OF THE MATTER IS THAT HE WAS SO DRUNK HE DIDN'T EVEN FEEL THE BUGS DRAINING HIS BLOOD OUT OF HIM...

THERE'S NO COUNT DRACULA AROUND HERE.

YOU MUST HAVE READ ONE OF MY CONCLUSIONS. PERHAPS IT'S A STRANGE DEATH, BUT IT'S BY NO MEANS SUPERNATURAL! A VAMPIRE?! NO WAY BOYS. JUST WAIT 'TIL I TELL YOUR MOTHERS...

43

THE END

SCRIPT
VIRGINIE VANHOLME
ILLUSTRATION
MAURICET

COLOURING LAURENT...

1 – THE VAMPIRE FROM THE MARSHES

COMING SOON

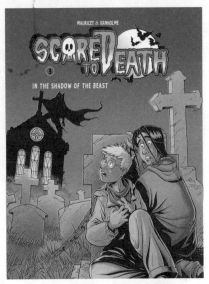

2 – MALEVOLENCE AND MANDRAKE

3 – IN THE SHADOW OF THE BEAST

9th CINEBOOK
The 9th Art Publisher

www.cinebook.com

SEE YOU SOON